Close Looks in a Spring Woods

Close Looks in a Spring Woods

MARTHA McKEEN WELCH

Dodd, Mead & Company • *New York*

For reviewing the text and photographs of this book the author would like to thank Jean Craighead George, Author, Naturalist; Mary-Ann Karpel, Ph.D., Consulting Entomologist, Brooklyn Botanic Gardens; Harold H. Clum, Ph.D., Consulting Botanist, Brooklyn Botanic Gardens.

Library of Congress Cataloging in Publication Data

Welch, Martha McKeen.
  Close looks in a spring woods.

  Summary: Describes the many changes that take place in the forest as winter is replaced by spring with its lengthening days and warming sun.

  1. Forest ecology —Juvenile literature. 2. Spring —Juvenile literature. [1. Spring. 2. Forest ecology. 3. Ecology] I. Title.
QH541.5.F6W425   574.5'2642   81-43218
ISBN 0-396-07998-9   AACR2

For "D" and for Mary

*L*ook at the woods in early March. Is everything dead?

No. Winter winds blew down trees, and old brown leaves cover the
ground. Bare branches are overhead, but living things are all around, safe
and waiting.

Millions of insect eggs are waiting. They were laid last year in many places. Some are on twigs and trees. Some are under logs and stones. Some are even underwater.

Birds that stayed in the woods through winter are waiting. Hungry deer are waiting, too. Good food is hard to find in winter.

Moss on the ground is waiting. It stays green in winter, but it doesn't grow. Underground, millions of seeds scattered last year are waiting. Seeds don't grow in winter, either. They wait in the frozen earth inside their protective covers.

Big thick roots that dig down deep are waiting. Smaller roots and bulbs
from which plants sprout year after year are also waiting underground.

flowering dogwood tree

shagbark hickory tree

Buds are waiting. They spent the winter tightly packed inside their waterproof coverings.
What is everything waiting for?

Waiting for the sun to warm the earth and for days that are longer and hotter. The sun's heat brings changes. Snow and ice melt. The ground begins to thaw.

Rain falls instead of snow. It drips from trees and soaks into the softening earth. Rain brings changes, too.

Carefully push away a few inches of soil, and you may find roots underground. The ones here are mayapple roots. Last fall the leaves on the mayapple plant died, but the roots did not. Tiny buds formed on them. They will grow upwards. New little roots will grow down. Be sure to cover them again with soil.

Near a stream, funny-looking pointed plants have already pushed through the softening earth. They grew from root clumps that waited all winter for the ground to unfreeze and for water to flow. Each curling hood protects a round ball dotted with tiny yellow flowers. Large leaves will grow later. They have a horrid smell if picked, so the plant is called skunk cabbage.

Pussy willow trees have also sucked up water and felt the warmth of the sun. Their flower buds swelled and burst their protective covers. Skunk cabbages and pussy willows bloom early as winter ends.

The days have been growing longer. About the twenty-first of March, the
hours of daylight and the hours of darkness are equal. This day is called the
equinox. It is also known as the first day of spring. But there are other
ways we can tell that spring has come to the woods.

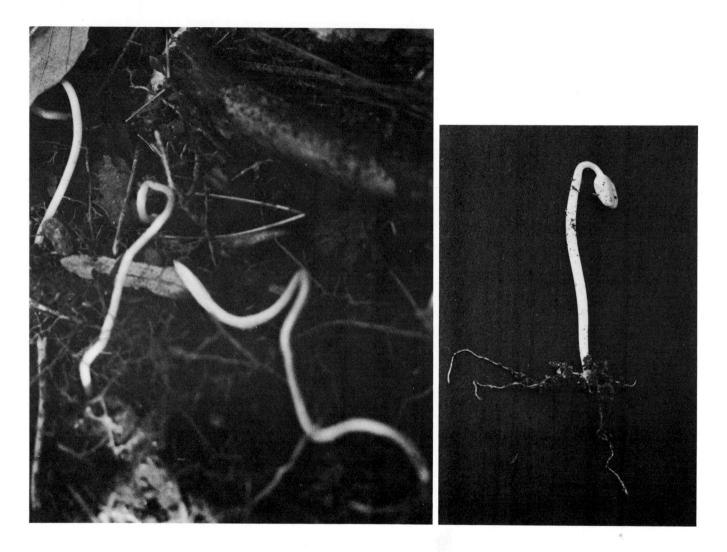

We know spring is here when seedlings have begun to sprout under the soil.

We know spring is here when a mayapple shoot has reached the light.

We know spring is here when the moss has started to grow. What grows on the moss looks almost like grass, but it isn't. What is it?

Near the moss, something else looks like a scary white ghost.

It is a baby fern, rolled tightly inside a woolly cover. It grew from a rootstock that may have been in the ground for nearly a hundred years. Uncoiling ferns resemble the curly ends of fiddles, so they are called "fiddleheads."

As warm spring days continue, leaves start growing on the skunk cabbage
by the stream. The flower balls and their pointed hoods have disappeared.
One plant close to the rushing water needs strong roots to hold tight.

Now there is a stem on the mayapple sprout. What is that on top? Will it be a leaf? Wait and see.

trout lily

false hellebore

violet

Other plants emerge from the earth. Each has its own kind of leaf.

27

Have you ever seen leaves like this? Each leaf is made up of three notched leaflets on a stem. In a week they will be green, but when they first appear they are bright red, inviting you to touch. But stay away. This is poison ivy.

Here is the mayapple again. The top is opening into a leaf that looks like a little umbrella.

trout lilies   *spring beauty*   *bloodroot*

More changes tell us spring has come. All sorts of woodland wild flowers bloom in April. They come up from bulbs, roots, and seeds that waited through the winter.

Dutchman's-breeches

violets

marsh marigolds

These early wild flowers need a lot of sun, so they bloom and produce their seeds before the woods gets shady.

31

The warm spring sun has aroused a yellow-spotted salamander. She has left her winter hole to look for water where she can find a mate and lay her eggs.

This is the woodland pond where she returns every spring. Two weeks after she lays her eggs, immature salamanders with gills will hatch and swim around. By late summer they will be full grown and have legs and lungs. Those that have not made meals for other water creatures will crawl onto land. There they will hibernate through the winter. Next spring they will lay their own eggs in the same pond. Some of them might live for twenty years.

Eggs are being laid in other places, too. A slug that passed the winter half-asleep under an old log has just laid some eggs. Can you find three? She will lay many more before next winter.

Now what is growing on the moss looks different. It is not grass at all, but delicate stems with tiny brown bags on top. Instead of making seeds, moss makes spores. When the bags pop open, ripe spores as fine as dust fall out to start new moss plants.

glistening ink caps

morels

Mushrooms grow from spores, too. Under the moist spring soil a spore sends out a thin thread, which spreads and branches as it grows. Baby mushrooms start to form on the mass of threads. They push up and continue growing above ground. Their caps are filled with spores, which will scatter and start new mushrooms.

It's snowing! In April? Will everything be ruined?

No. The next day is warm. Spring snow melts quickly. The moisture will
help things grow.

The ferns are all right.

columbine

The wild flowers are all right. The moss is all right.

40

The mayapples are just fine.

Trees use water from the melted snow. Their roots suck it up from the earth and send it to the branches, where buds are beginning to grow fat and open. Some buds contain flowers, which make seeds for new trees. The flower bud on a dogwood tree looks like a tiny cup full of eggs.

red maple blossom

birch tree catkin

Flowers on the birch tree are called "catkins." Scarlet flower blossoms on the red maple tree bring color to the awakening woods.

Some buds contain leaves, which use sunlight to make food for the tree.
This leaf bud on a shagbark hickory tree looks ready to burst.

When it opens, the delicate leaves inside begin to grow. Leaf buds all through the woods are unfolding.

Soon the dogwood trees are in full bloom, a sure sign that May has come.

A dogwood blossom looks like one flower with four petals. But the "petals" are really the bud's protective covers, folded all the way back. The real flowers will open from the cluster of buds at the center. They will make bright red fruits by fall.

Under the dogwood tree a rabbit sits perfectly still when it sees you.

But it is not perfectly still on the oak tree. Hundreds of tiny gypsy moth caterpillars are wiggling all around. Long days and warm temperatures caused them to hatch from their egg case. They will live in the trees and swing on silken threads. After growing and shedding their skins about six times, they will be nearly two inches long. Gypsy moth caterpillars harm trees by eating millions of leaves. They themselves make delicious meals for birds and mice.

Long days and warm temperatures also brought an ugly water nymph out on a nearby fern. It had been growing and shedding its skin in the water for more than a year. But now the nymph is just an empty shell. What came out of it?

A beautiful shining dragonfly. It pulled itself out of a slit in the nymph shell, dried off in the sun, and flew away. A dragonfly rests with its four transparent wings spread open. It zips through the air with its six legs formed into a basket, catching mosquitoes and other insects as it flies.

This iridescent blue damselfly also left an empty nymph shell somewhere near the water. It holds its dark wings tight together when it rests.

Meanwhile, stink bugs have been laying eggs on a leaf. The stink bugs stayed in the ground through winter and part of spring. But now the leaves they need for food and for egg-laying are out. In five or six days, baby stink bugs will hatch. Each one will be smaller than the head of a pin.

Seeds have now formed on the trout lilies, and on the other early wild flowers.

yellow lady's-slipper

jack-in-the-pulpit

Solomon's seal

Since the leaves on trees are fully opened, wild flowers that need shade are blooming or starting to make their seeds.

Look.

A mayapple flower. It has a deep yellow center surrounded by shining white petals.

Hidden under their roof of little umbrellas is a whole secret woods full of mayapple flowers.

This one is yours to watch.

Spring is ending, but a new mayapple fruit is beginning. It will ripen during the summer and then spread its seeds. During fall and winter, the seeds will wait in the ground. Then, when the sun warms the earth and soft rains fall, the mayapple seeds will start to sprout. Old mayapple roots will send out shoots and we will know that spring has come again.

But now green leaves cover the ground. Everything looks fresh and new.
Plants are busy growing, blooming, making their seeds. Woodland animals
have plenty of food.

A big green canopy of leaves is overhead, filled with the songs of nesting birds. It will keep the woods cool during the hot summer days to come.

Index

Birch tree catkin, 43
Birds, 10
Bloodroot, 30
Buds, 13, 42-45, 47

Columbine, 40

Damselfly, 52
Deer, 10
Dogwood, 46; flower bud, 42, 47
Dragonfly, 50-51
Dutchman's-breeches, 31

Eggs, insect, 9; slug, 34
Equinox, 19

False hellebore, 27
Ferns, 24, 39

Glistening ink caps, 36

Gypsy moth caterpillars, 49

Insects, 49, 50-52; eggs, 9

Jack-in-the-pulpit, 55

Marsh marigolds, 31
Mayapple, 16, 21, 26, 29, 41, 56
Morels, 36
Moss, 11, 22, 35, 40
Mushrooms, 36

Poison ivy, 28
Pussy willow, 16

Rabbit, 48
Rain, 15
Red maple flower bud, 43
Roots, 12; mayapple, 16;
    skunk cabbage, 25

Salamander, yellow-spotted,
    32-33
Seedlings, 20
Seeds, 11, 54
Shagbark hickory leaf bud, 44-45
Skunk cabbage, 17, 25
Slug, 34
Snow, 37
Solomon's seal, 55
Spores, 35, 36
Spring beauty, 30
Stink bugs, 53

Trout lily, 27, 30, 54

Violets, 31

Wild flowers, 30-31, 40, 54-55

Yellow lady's-slipper, 55